Living with Splinters

Lovanda Brown

Copyright © 2016 Lovanda Brown
All rights reserved.
ISBN: 0692809546
ISBN-13: 978-0692809549

"This is *precisely* the time when artists go to work. There is no time for despair, no place for self-pity, no need for silence, no room for fear. We speak, we write, we do language. That is how civilizations heal."

-Toni Morrison

Table of Contents

I. Rocks and Gravel *(For Jamaica)*

    1. Rocky Roads   6

    2. All Ready   7

    3. Burying Marley   8

    4. Words I still Remember   9

II. Stained Cement *(For Bridgeport)*

    5. For Bridgeport   11

    6. Remember   12

    7. Remains   13

III. Living with Splinters *(For Me)*

    8. Inkless Pen   15

    9. Everything   16

    10. Love Happened to Me   18

    11. When Your Hand is Left Suspended in the Air   19

    12. All that is Responsibility   20

    13. When Your Hand is Left Suspended in the Air   21

    14. Stream of Light   22

    15. When Your Hand is Left Suspended in the Air   24

    16. Blind Justice   25

IV. Remembering the Decayed *(For Them)*

    17. Beneath (For Maya Angelou)   29

    18. He Sleeps (For Blaine)   31

    19. Finding the 'Write' Words (For You)
        32

    20. On the Morning of 9/11   33

V. Cracked Enamel *(For YOU)*

    21. Because I'm Happy   35

    22. Groundhog   36

    23. Just Say No   36

    24. Caught   37

    25. Enlightened   37

    26. Heavenly Father, I Feel You...   38

    27. I-95   38

    28. Things People Say when They're Bored or Misguided   39

    29. We Need to Talk   40

    30. Things that Excite Me   41

    31. Dear Mind   42

PART I.
ROCKS and Gravel
(For Jamaica)

Rocky Roads

I smell the scent of burning animal flesh.
They tied up wailing goats and severed each head
For dinner, the goats were cleanly eviscerated.
I ate all that was placed in front of me.
The cows which hid in bushes and sticks were saved
For last. After all, we needed milk each morning.
I hardly take time to recount the steps I've taken:
I remember those chipped red steps I trotted,
My face had fell upon them times too many;
Yet still, I hopped on each step, every day and night.
The steps led to broken and uneven roads
But still, we walked with bare and uncovered feet.
As children, we knew and thought of nothing—
We cantered down rocky roads and lived
in Jamaica's rural streets.

All Ready

I'd stop to entertain this if I had
not heard it already. I'm steady
straight towards school corridors
filled with apathetic faces and a few
secret whores who could care less than
a dime that "Ole' Miss Shine lose di man
fi di third time." I've heard this already
along with nine questions short of the 21 quota.
 You got me. I'm caught.
 I could absolutely care more about who told her.
"Yeh, mi a leff out fi school now." As if
the largest clue wasn't screaming at you
in the form of a fully loaded back pack
 slapped on burdened shoulders—both hands filled
with multicolored folders almost left in haste.
I'd stop to talk if I had not acquired the taste of this.
I simply have no time for this. "Yes Lawd, mi late now.
Time gone an mi still deh ya. Unno fava!"
 I run before the slammed door to leave you all
with this I am sure—discussing "di same woman
unno did a chat bout before."
You knew I'd leave this way. You knew I
had nothing to say. Afta all—wi do dis nuff time
already.

Burying Marley

Here's an ode to slaying stereotypes:
The products of imagination too sublime.
Today, I kill the dreaded weed-smoker--
Today, I shift this paradigm.
The products of imagination too sublime
Have Marley-ed the average Jamaican,
But today I shift this paradigm.
Today I kill the undying refrain "Yeh, man"
Marley is now the average Jamaican
Posthumously surviving in us all.
Today I kill his undying refrain, "yeh, man"--
Ash out the ganja once and for all.
 As he survives posthumously through us,
We strive to be remembered ourselves.
Ash out the ganja image once and for all--
Tread the labels given to us by all else.
As we strive to be remembered ourselves,
We band to kill the dreaded weed smoker.
And tread the labels given to us by everyone else---
Here's an ode to burying stereotypes.

Words I Still Remember

All of the words you let travel,
A cruel path you let them take,
Have taunted my every move,
And moves I have yet to make,
Have matured into a ruthless fire
Growing brighter than glowing ember;
All of the words you said to me
That day,
Are words I still remember.
You left an awful bitter taste—
Condemned me to my wheeling hearse
Hateful words you let me keep,
which I deem my lonely curse,
And all the words you have forgotten--
Time has cooled your chilling temper,
Are words I have yet to let go
Are words I still remember.
You wanted me dead that day,
it seems,
You held no censorship.
You attacked by all impartial means,
Let war seep from your lips.
Ammunition you had in store for me
A vengeful wrath
You made me render.
And all the words
You didn't say
Are
Words
I
Still
Remember.

PART II.
STAINED Cement
(For Bridgeport)

For Bridgeport

Bottles roll aimlessly—kicked to collect
Dirt shamelessly. Roads licked with grime
And grit, colored shirts have codes, stained pits
Collared dogs wail sirens' song—exist to haunt
and carry on. We fail to hear the crying men
locked in by wire, shut in again as blaring music
Invades the streets, we're mocked and crushed
By wealthy beasts. Unless each heavy gun unloads
You'll never hear the stories told of stealthy moms
with deafened sons who sever odds, who don't out-run
the expectations placed on them to join the mass of
crying men and even then it's quite the same
they barely seem to know our names. Each set of
reps hold signs poised high and ink their faces
for those who die, they mourn young boys
and take them too, by storm they claim each
avenue. The bridge it shakes. Why won't it stretch
 to save the penniless, ranting wretch?
Who sleeps beneath the bridge's port,
and waves for chance of some comfort.
He sits in cave, he rocks and chants "they never
got to see me dance." And while the dreams
of college fail, and seams of bonds
grow weak and frail, tears rarely meet the
 ground; the babies hardly make a sound. There is no
option, we have no vote, there is no room
upon the boat. Some live assuaged by vain belief
they live content with state's relief. Some don
uniforms with fast-food stench hell bent on saving
to mock the wretch. But for those who fail to conform
Destined to conquer the flailing worm
They simply refuse to live with doubts,
 they live to tell—
they make it out.

Remember

I've walked the streets and traced the parts you left
Behind. The blood still stains the concrete, the spray
Paint both dimmed and dried. I watched you leave and wept.
The old yellow hydrant still stands. Defiant, it proudly stays
To retell the stories you failed to keep each time it grows wet.
The grass is still green too, though I'm sure you knew I'd say
That it's home to the critters we'd watch dance, caterpillars that crept.
The blades of green still move by blow. I still watch them sway.

At night the porch lights drive the darkness further into the night;
The old man flings rocks when I disturb the silence,
And because I can hardly respect it when he isn't in sight
I invade with noise, stomp the yards--forsake all shyness.

I walk the streets and remember it all without you.
You'd be surprised to know which parts forgot you too.

Remains

I can only recall one summer
Spent there. Though exactly where

Cannot be recounted by those
Who led me. Faint and faded remains

Of those shabby doors, lollipops—red
Bicycles and wooden floors

Creeps in with the faint scent of cut grass.
I'd return and re-burn chopped wood, centered

Amidst indiscernible faces, if I could,
But I can't. The posted signs poised

Stealthily along the journey there, signs
I once studied to condense the time and

The lengthy trip has blurred in with
Rosy cheeks. Now all I have is this.

This feeble attempt to reunite scattered
pieces of an exhumed labyrinth. Still,

the decay is too far-gone. I hardly recognize
any of it any more. River banks and clear

blue skies are all I can see clearly, yet
The longing for what and who I can't recollect

 still remains alongside the remains of this puzzle.
Its immortality will sustain long after I am gone.

Part III.
LIVING with Splinters
(For Me)

Inkless Pen

I've adapted quite well to loneliness--just enough
To hold not one single regard for despair.
It's been long since I've trotted along the lines of love;
It's been long since my words have found air.
Yet I find this old chair forces me to consider
The blank page I've left neglected for too long.
My words have grown both aged and embittered
And not one of them seems to belong.

I've outgrown the resentment I used to feel
And I've since prayed through feelings I couldn't bear.
Now I am cured of shouldering all too much
I've grown apathetic to the world and its cares.

But here I still sit pondering, waiting to be found
By the words that left me—
left me to drown.

Everything

God,
 I remember everything—
All of the things careless shoulders
shrug off.
I remember what was
said to me
And how her tone
made me soft.
I remember the story
the sky told,
and how the rain
mimicked my pain,
Of all the stories I let
grow old;
The stories I left to stain.
And now since it's seems
You've overlooked
my tears and offering,
I thought I should tell you
before I go,
that I remember
Everything.
I remember when I was obedient
And they all shamed me.
Words I can't begin to utter
are what they all named me.
I remember when I cried to you,
And you didn't hear a thing.
I promise you,
I just so happen to
remember
Everything.
I remember who was there,
but I remember who was not.

I remember when he left to meet you—
A time they all forgot.
I remember my dangling hope
and when they came to cut the string
And just so they know
who they are,
Just know,
I remember
Everything.
I remember going to altar
and displacing it from my chest.
I remember how I wept each night—
How I longed to find some rest.
I remember frozen shoulders
poised against me
as if I had nothing to bring,
and today I thought
I'd remind them all
that I remember
Everything.
If this has taught me anything
I know only You can offer bliss,
That compassion as I have come to show,
doesn't even exist.
I've learned the world keeps turning
Despite my haunting pain,
People are learning to pray for the world,
Links are broken throughout the chain.
Yet before I join the mass of those
Who still have life to sing,
I thought I'd tell you
Although you have forgotten,
That I remember
Everything.

Love Happened to Me

And he loved me
with unsentimental deception,
like a devil's spawn—
relentlessly pandering
to my weaknesses and most profound
insecurities.
He loved me
with sadistic obsession
like a pedophile engaging in child's play—
It's unnerving yet compelling,
for the audience,
as the act of causing such damage becomes
a game of foreign understanding;
the mind refuses to waive its curiosity
until the meaning is grasped.
And in the most perilous way,
He loved me.
But like a provoked braid
I was unraveling.
Crumbling before my very eyes
was my disinterred heart
left carelessly alongside
my sleeve's surface;
it shakily stood frail and
unprotected.
Because,
you see,
I didn't happen
to fall in love;
love happened to me.
And I still cannot
understand
why?

When Your Hand is Left Suspended in the Air and it Noticeably Goes Unnoticed

I've been catching fleeting
Remnants of cotton with
One palm and his darker side
For the past three minutes.
Suspension. Joints lock to form
Erection. Here it stands.
Eyes gloss over. Points are made.
Redundantly, of course. But now
I am lost. Uneasy. If the gesture
Is broken, its splinters will puncture
My pride. For the hand still stands
Noticeably unnoticed.
I resort to desperate measures
To ease my humiliation. I recite
My logic quietly to ensure it still
Holds validity. I know they can see
My ears overheating. But the silent
Palm refuses to wave for help.
Rollercoasters. I've resorted to
Rollercoasters now. A familiar ride
That welcomes the rise of one palm
And its sympathetic partner.

All that is Responsibility

I put on my purple onesie. You
Put on your green one. I put on
Animated past time. You put on
Attention. I put 30 seconds
On soggy waffles. You put on
The syrup. I put on pursuing coyotes.
You put on talking dogs. You hear shuffling
Outside the door. I hear pieces of metal
Meet. Mailbox is full. I put on worry.
You put on stress. I turn off sound.
You put on pants. I take off youth.
You take yours off too. Peace apocalypse.
I put on fear. You put on acceptance.
We put on age once more.
The waffles are cold.

When Your Hand is Left Suspended in the Air and it Noticeably Goes Unnoticed

Once both shoulders are restrained.
Left resting on hard metal. You'll notice
There's still enough room
For both hands to touch sky.
Those sitting before you seem ready.
Those seated behind you sound afraid.
Palms clutch the locked embrace.
They're only modest until
The whirlwind begins.
Once the world beneath
Is reduced to an ant farm.
Both palms hover over flailing locks.
And the surrounding witnesses
Still fail to note that your
Palms have defied gravity
with each twisting turn.
They're waving now too.

The Stream of Light

The day always comes with more than mere light
still the invasive stream of light between partially closed shutters provokes it all
by streaming thoughts of stress and panic while pacing on worn nerves
and my need for REM-staged sleep sneaks in the startling stream so then

I bury my head in fluffed feather sacks to appease my awaking frustration and
inevitably, the burgeoning list of obligations comes streaming down the current
which is when I officially lose whatever is left of my wilted sanity and
I reveal one eye to the suspended air still afraid to glance at time's reminder.

Both of my legs rest unmoved beneath tousled covers as I struggle to face the time when a thought streams in…

How bland are these walls? I don't have the time to cover them for
the pale green has long-since lost its appeal, yet that doesn't shake my stare or the steam because
now all I remember is breakfast, work, and more work and I simply can't handle this today—
Where is my phone? I glide my hand over the empty space beside me and then

Another stream of light has made its way into the current
And finds settlement on the face of the clock—
Dammit it's 8 AM
and I still
Can't find my phone.

A fallen pillow reveals the phone's hiding place and now

The bright-lit screen assuages my worn nerves reminding
me that it...is...only...Saturday.
Suddenly, both legs find strength as I run over to the
shutters' place and join once segregated curtains.
The stream is no more and its current has calmed.
I'm going back to bed.

When Your Hand is Left Suspended in the Air and it Noticeably Goes Unnoticed.

The surrounding screams blend
Like music. Stimulating the beat
Already streaming. The melodies
Bathe tense shoulders and build
A scene of euphoric vertigo.
The lit stage ahead releases unifying
Contentment.
That's when the muscles react.
They lift each arm higher
And force them to keep
Courage. Humiliation shared.
To sway along with blazing
Lighters and nodding heads.
Basking away in accepted
Conspicuous invisibility.

Blind Justice

Oh, to be heard in a crowded room
Where anger and sadness grow,
Where wounded men cry aloud,
Mothers mourn sons they have yet
To know.
Deep in a small corner, you'll find me,
Armed with pen in hand
With pieces in bosom and tear-stained
cheeks,
I note the fall of man.
And now we can't be silenced
We've called the marching band.
They took the broom, called us "free"
And left us with the pan.
We've walked a splintered path.
We've held hands in cold march.
Attended sacred places
They said were too much for us.
We've sent harsh Jimmy packing--
used his heat to comb our hair,
We found a place to vent
And then
We gave them room to share.
And while we've replaced
Woven ropes with frost and
cried, "we're free!"
Our sons lay nameless,
On cold pavements,
Blood stains outline our streets.
We've flaunted wealth
And in bad health
We put away our hymns
They gave us the rope
Of the mic and told us,

"Go 'head, sing!"
They even kept us fooled
inside
the "master's" West Wing!
And we married their women
In vain belief
That "justice" can see
Anything.
The food is brought to us now
and the cotton clothes our backs.
Frightened by all the things we own,
we don't consider all we lack.
And now they've come
To take our sons
We have no where to hide!
We failed to see the signs were flailing--
That we we took it all in stride.
And now they say,
"You've done enough,
You've nothing left to bring.
O wise little negro
Our "justice" can't see
a dime worth anything."
A pain is buried in my chest
Of all they had to take.
Our sons and brothers
Had to perish to shake us all
Awake,
But since we are all here
In this room,
I thought I'd finally share.
I don't speak unless I'm given space,
so I'd like to make this clear.
I know the truth has a way of hurting,
but I'm prepared to let this sting,
We must wipe the veil from our eyes—

Unite in full upswing
Because I know the checkered palms
clasping hand in hand
Have been so comforting,
I need you to know,
for what it's worth
"Their justice?"
Can't see
any
thing.

PART IV.
REMEMBERING the Decayed
(For Them)

Beneath
For Maya Angelou (1928-2014)

I know why the crow has
landed beneath your feet
Ms. Marguerite.
There was little left
you could do.
Women have risen phenomenally
Men still wonder
Because of you.
Tragedy acquired
 Its own twist of fate
As time would have it
Its favor rested on
A bright-eyed face
And on the pulse
Of that morning,
Still
Even then you rose,
To refuse the cackling
calling
Of the blackened crows.
They struggled to understand
How?
 yet we know why.
We've harkened to the wisdom
Your hand has left
Behind.
Old folks laughed, kind
Enough to share
The messages,
The pearls
All the nuggets they could find.
And then one darkening day
In the oddest of time
The end of May,

The crows flocked together
To kill the shine
And take you, Ms. 'Rite
Away.
Yet they couldn't lift
All they hoped to bear.
Only your body failed
to resist defeat,
And that is why
My dear Ms. 'Rite
The cackling, blackened
And tackling crow
Could only land,
Beneath your feet.

He Sleeps
For Blaine (1987-2003)

Soft prints work to glide over tiled keys
both salted and peppered in tradition;

I am lost by the leading of chimed voices
and before I can find my way, I am led directly

to him. Trained teeth assembled beneath
bulging pink lips, somehow, seem to

find me first, and the rhythm in my chest
forgets it song until it is seasoned in sharp chords

and the pain creates a new beat. His suit
mimics the tradition and beneath it is cold flesh

that burns to embrace for too long. Moist drops
fall to thaw its biting sting, and they continue

for quite some time until both eyes
are milked tirelessly. The soft prints lose

their grace as aggression meets grievous tones
tremoring with each strike, and all is given

until they softly turn to bid adieu. He fades with
each passing note and I am left to wait for him
as he sleeps.

Finding The 'Write' Words

There's a kind of poem addressed to you
Anonymously, and yet I haven't found it.
Traced throughout it are all the words you said
And all the words you didn't. You said you loved me—
Well, that's in there too. Vividly recorded like
The mic carried by a singing violin. Childhood nostalgia
Of Chewed barbies and daffodils can only do but so much.
We haven't bonded over our youth in years.
The memories we shared were removed and tousled
like a dishwasher's picnic. But here I am, replaying those words,
 waiting for them to find place in another's hand—
For that unknown poem addressed to you,
to leak beyond the smooth tip of another's pen.
For this poem to come and address me, every now
And again. But like you, it never comes,
and I still wait.

On the Morning of 9/11

The traffic chased behind due time,
Disgruntled chatter filled the space,
Good mothers cared as they always did,
The events before were all erased
By those who worked in careless bane,
The buildings—crashed by eager planes,
And took the mothers' breath away,
The traffic chasers couldn't stay,
Disgruntled chatter turned to screams,
The twins were torn right from the seams,
Today, we now know what it means
To embrace each yesterday.

PART V.
CRACKED Enamel
(For YOU)

Because I'm Happy

I've decided that this lurking sadness--
Depression seeking to take me under
And snip what is left of my dangling hope
Can quite frankly go kick rocks.
I'm happy dammit.
Pharell reminds me all the time.
I'm so happy that Julie Andrews
Is singing again.
I am eternally amused
By absolutely nothing. This smile
Is frickin' permanent, and my
Pretend Uncle Eddie Murphy and his 52
Teeth couldn't be more unknowingly proud.
I'm happier than what it really means to be gay.
I'm so happy that Hostess' Twinkies gave up on everyone,
And came back months later just for me.
(You're welcome.)
And even if I'm not
Because let's face it,
Life is hardly amusing,
I stand here absolutely refusing
To find comfort in shrouded windows,
Little Debbie and re-runs of Titanic.
So today, I'll pretend that Rose moved her
Selfish ass over and helped Jack on the door.
Today, Robin Williams is still very much alive.
Today I am actually a frugal millionaire
Who has decided to test the waters of a struggling
Post-grad student.
Today I'm happy,
whether I believe it or not.

High-Cools...

Groundhog

I saw a groundhog
So where the hell is spring? Is
That not how this works?

Just Say No

I ate food last night
It just won't stay down there, man.
Say no to old milk.

Caught

When did you get here?
How long have you been watching?
It's not what you think.

Enlightened

I want to be rich.
So I don't need my degrees?
And you share this now?

Heavenly Father, I Feel you…

God's thoughts of me, now:
How on earth did I make her?
Let us start from scratch!

I-95

Stay in your lane, please!
I don't think you wave like that.
I can not hear you.

Things People Say when They're Bored or Misguided

I'm hungry. Or at least I ate
An hour ago. Why on earth
Haven't you called me? Have I
Bored you in some way?
Whatever. I'm hungry.
I need new friends. No one's interesting.
The television is a wasted invention.
I should be a producer.
I'm chock full of bad ideas.
Bathing monkeys. Kissing hyenas.
What time is it anyway?
I'm hungry.

"We" Need to Talk?

Here's the thing:
do not tell me
that "we need to talk"
with a hardened face
determined to scold me
about things
that don't affect me.
What you mean
to say
is that you need
to talk,
and you need me
to listen.
Now that we have that
established—
Proceed.
The moment is yours.

Things that Excite Me

God
Kids reading
Reality show cancellations
Buckling ankles over platform heels
Widely inappropriate inclinations
Understanding the joke
Blissfully watching you miss the joke
All things creative
Not being broke
The first signs of winter
Getting ready for winter
Getting warm during winter
Challenging the point of winter
Buying shoes
Watching my collection grow
Finding perfect excuses to buy more
Knowing things most people don't know
Writing
Loathing all first drafts
Praising all final drafts
Sharing them with the world
Second chances
Exercising twisted humor
Laughing at myself before you do.

Dear Mind

Dear Mind, I love you. You separate me
From the raging idiotic to the

Mind-numbingly dunce brains
All the time. And for that,

I thank you. This ode is owed.
You're not perfect. I know that.

In fact, you're the reason I know that—
Look at how humble you are.

You have to work out a few things though.
You bring up things that make it hard for me to be

A decent human being on a daily basis,
but I love you even when you force me to cackle

At the misfortune of others. God bless you.
You're great in that way.

Now there are bigger mentals out there,
So try to stay in your lane. Math isn't your thing.

I get that. Don't think too hard about it.
Just let it go. You know you plus writing

Makes awesome literature babies.
Take pride in that. Not everyone has mastered

The art of equivocation. Oh yes!
And thank you for getting me through college.

How the hell did you pull that off?

Always thinking. You have that whole

Memorizing thing in the bag now.
It took us awhile, but we got there.

I just wanted to let you know
That I appreciate you and that is why

I've subscribed to both Netflix and Hulu.
It's all for you, babe. You deserve it.

www.ingramcontent.com/pod-product-compliance
Lightning Source LLC
Chambersburg PA
CBHW031943070426
42450CB00006BA/870